reflections of winter

photography
by don werner

poetry
by joyce teichner garrett

Holt, Rinehart and Winston
New York

Published simultaneously in Canada by Holt, Rinehart and Winston of Canada, Limited.

Library of Congress Cataloging in Publication Data

Werner, Donald L.
    Reflections of winter.

1. Photography - Landscapes. 2. Winter - Poetry. I Garrett, Joyce Teichner. II Title.
TR660.5.W47   779'.092'4   78-55454
ISBN Hardbound: 0-03-044981-2
ISBN Paperback: 0-03-044986-3

FIRST EDITION

PRINTED IN THE UNITED STATES OF AMERICA
10 9 8 7 6 5 4 3 2 1

How do a photographer and a poet create a visual and verbal essence?
Walking the streets in winter, the special beauty of snow light on city
forms, the delicate, infinitely varied grays, the soft massed forms welded
into a dreamlike atmosphere, became for the photographer, Don Werner,
the focus of his personal vision.

Opening us to another level of consciousness, into an environment of
half-remembered dreams become tangible, Don's camera reveals a muted
graphic beauty.

The photographs are full negative and are born in the camera. Instanta-
neous recognition and response create the statement. Expertise has freed
Don from mechanical dependence—mind and eye work together to select
the gestalt of a view. This is how he makes an imprint—this is his way.

Because of his background as a painter, another dimension is added to his
work. This discipline, especially in watercolor, which requires much the
same decision in action, allows him fluidity of choice, enriching the
texture of his photographs. Don is a native of California (an environment
which has many links to the Orient) and he immersed himself in studies of
Asian and Western art and design. It was in Korea, however, as an artist,
that he had the opportunity to live in this great culture, and it was in
Korea, too, among the terraced rice fields and mountain shrines, that he
first saw the magic and mystery of falling snow.

We are enhanced by sharing the fantasy and beauty that the artist has
given us, which took a special dedication and sensitivity to reveal.

I the poet grew up in a suburban city, where the uniformity of my street
was offset by the imagination of a wealthy neighbor who created an
authentic Japanese garden on her grounds. Shrines, lanterns, flowers and
shrubs, and above all a wonderful red, arching bridge over a stream—here
I spent many, many hours.

Recognizing the same elements in Don's pictures, as I had felt in all forms
of Oriental art, I reacted to his perceptions in a deeply personal way. My
poems grew spontaneously from the intimate beauty of the photography.

Joyce Teichner Garrett

I see designs and patterns.

Photography is a door to seeing life—its memories and its dreams.

Through the lens of my camera space and time
coalesce and Winter is transmuted into "Reflections
of Winter."

in the silent

city

covered,

I hear snow

fall

afterwards

this remains,

a

rippled shadow

and

the silent

block of

still life

I cannot see

the footsteps

that once led

to my apartment door.

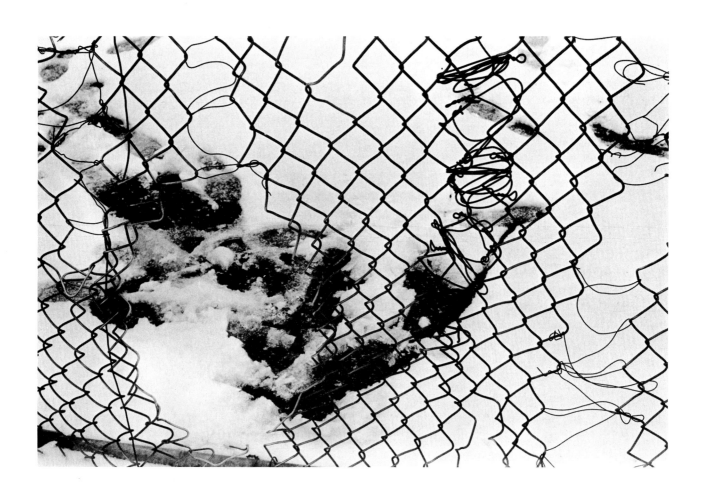

the sun

moves across

these

gray faces

throwing shadows

on fissures

of fire escapes.

the fence is

a boundary,

but the links

take us to

another world.

I enjoy sharing visual surprises.

Sudden revelations of light and shade, shape and
texture excite me.

Linear rhythms are paths for the eye.

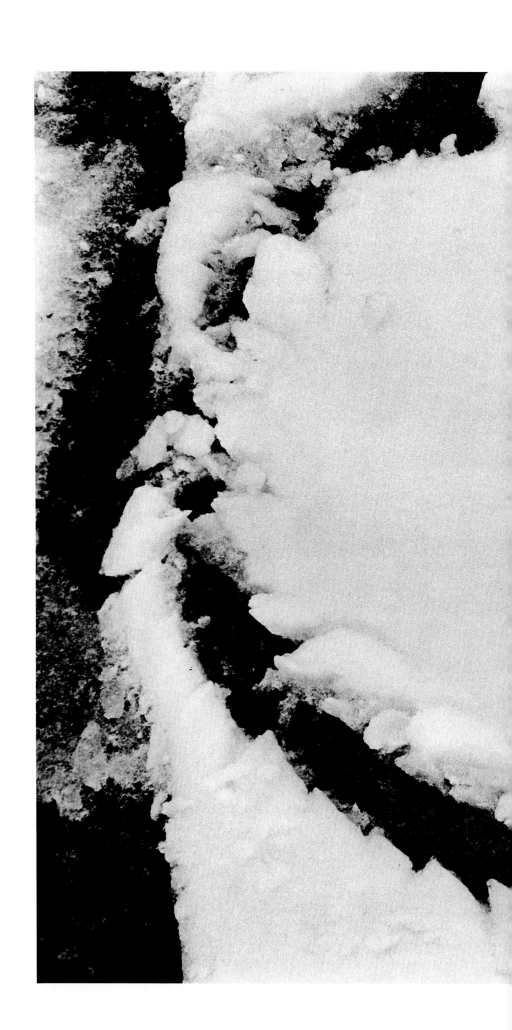

the sphere of…

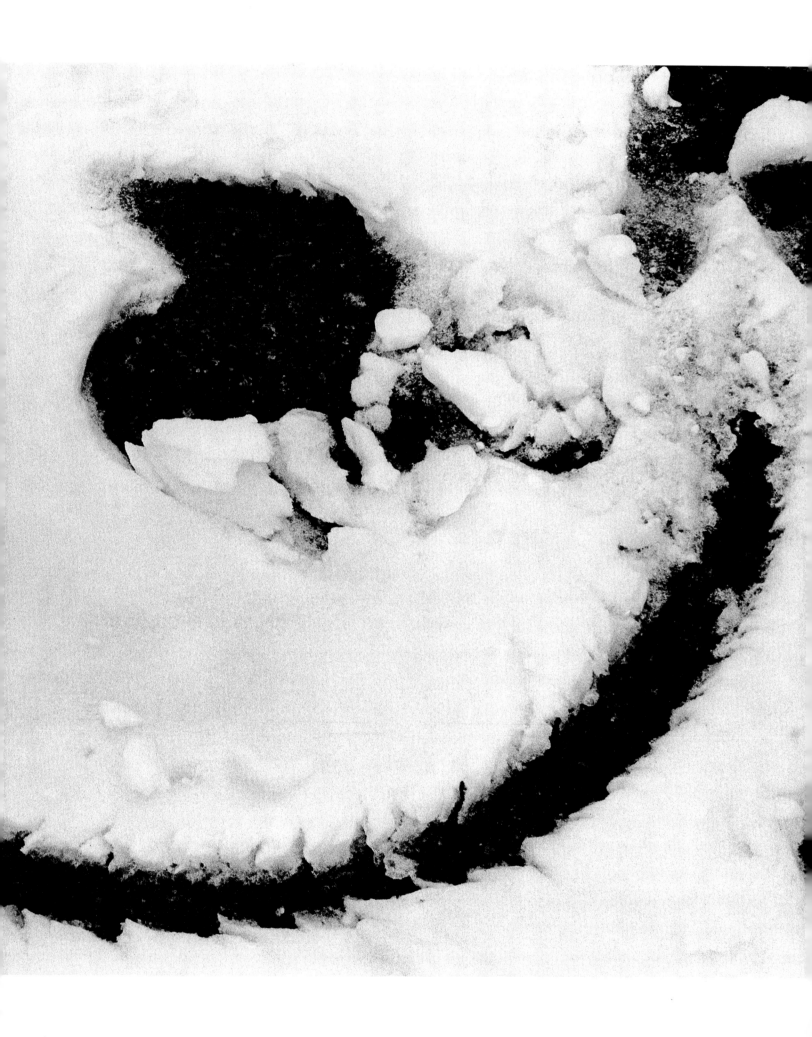

paths

is

not

broken

who painted

this tree?

where am I
to place a
step,
in crossing
this tangled fence?

*KUSA-MAKURA**

black hair

of

sumi-e,

now

you grow old –

shades of

gray begin to tell

of your journey.

*title is from
Soseki Natsume's book,*
The Three Cornered World

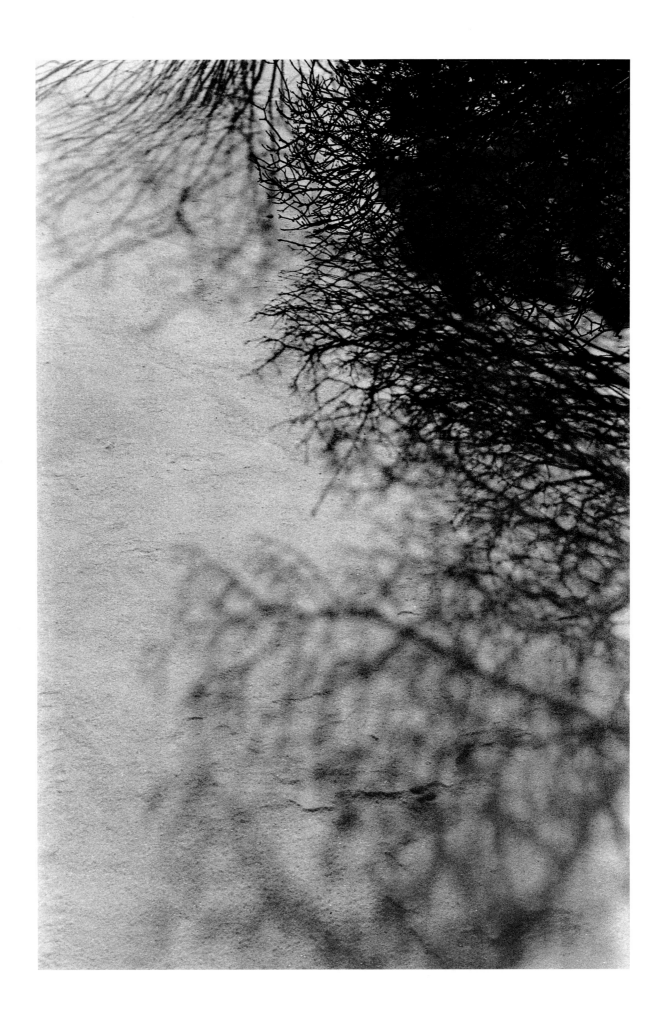

Deliberate designs and patterns become happenings.

going

someplace,

it

does not

matter...

where.

to amble or

float…

still I am

someplace.

I select a subject for its design possibilities and for
what it expresses of life and the evidence of life.

I am forced to look, to see; and the sights
are full of beauty.

A scene changes, varying as light itself. Addition and subtraction of light sculptures the world around us.

Snow is a special delight, transforming a world.

I followed

another's

path

for this

promenade,

yet

can you tell?

my steps are

hidden,

but there.

We see in color. Blacks and whites are a complete palette in themselves. Absence of color has its own strength, subtlety and nuance.

the

flower of…

an expanse:

sol'tude

no words

yet

snow speaks,

but

we

do not know

if

the dog,

the person

wanted

this

stillness

before bird's

dip into

her

watery reflection.

the dancers'

echoed

reflection

of and

from

water:

back

to water.

"More" can be abundance of detail

or an essence of detail.

alone

contemplating

my life-

comforted by my life.

and my eye in winter recalls soft, quiet, elegant glistenings.

Winter's quiet

is melting,

drifting

away

when

does

my shadow

become

my signature?

of

different

roots

yes–

but,

one family.

how far
do
I
run,
do
I flow…
where
do I go?

before

you go,

let me

once more

bow down,

touch

your cool skin,

to remember

this

sweet touch.

summer

comes

too fast.

a boat

the

person

floating down

the river

waking

sleeping

passing out

of sight.

I believe in painting,

    in photography,

in memories and dreams.

the sphere

of

paths

does not

break:

all

is recalled,

all continues.

PHOTOGRAPHER'S COMMENTS

All the pictures were taken in and around Manhattan, especially Central Park and Riverside Park. They express and at the same time transcend the urban environment.

My chief reason for photographing this aspect of the city is a result of a preconception. Before coming here, I believed that New York City was a dehumanized place of steel, glass and concrete; that the sky was hidden by tall buildings and that indeed only one tree grew, and that was in Brooklyn. It is amazing how differently one feels after living here—the canyons of Wall Street are not the entire city; what a relief it is to find nature shining through.

Winter is a special time when the busy frenetic world of sounds, anxieties and confusion is muffled. I can see and feel the snow fall, and in my camera capture those beautiful moments in time and light as visual shorthand.

While I was in Korea and Japan I seriously began to use a camera as an extension to my painting. It was while traveling the countryside, visiting temples and mountain shrines and viewing Oriental gardens of perfect proportion and continuity that my esthetic developed.

Snow brings to our city a simplicity and purity of delineated beauty that is closest to my memories of Oriental landscape.

COLOPHON

CREATED, PHOTOGRAPHED AND DESIGNED BY DON WERNER

TITLE: ZOPPO REGULAR

TEXT: STATEMENTS, CENTURY EXPANDED

POETRY: CENTURY ITALICS

PAPER: WARRENS FLO COAT

PRINTING: HALLIDAY LITHOGRAPH, PLYMPTON, MASSACHUSETTS

PLATES: BY LASER SCANNING

BLACK AND WHITE REPRODUCTIONS PRODUCED AT STUDIO
ANALYSIS UNDER THE PERSONAL SUPERVISION OF PAOLO
RIPOSIO, TORINO, ITALY, REPRESENTED IN THE UNITED
STATES BY OFFSET SEPARATIONS CORPORATION, NEW YORK

PHOTOGRAPHS PRINTED FOR BOOK: JANE HAMBORSKY

MECHANICALS: DIANE WASSERMAN

COORDINATED BY: LOIS de la HABA

ACKNOWLEDGMENTS

Many of the images were first exhibited at the Parrish Museum, Southampton, Long Island, New York under the directorship of Jean Weber. I thank Jean for her friendship and encouragement, and the excellent opportunity to see the works hanging together. It was from this exhibition that the germ of a possible book grew.

I also thank Pamela Landgraff, Director of the Greenburgh Nature Center, Scarsdale, New York and Andrew Maass, Director of the Fresno Arts Center, who also believed in and exhibited the work.

I am especially appreciative of the late Axel Grosser, an exceptionally sensitive photographer, printer and artist.

My thanks to Joyce Teichner Garrett for her lovely insightful poetry; to my friends Frank Kozelek, James Prescott, Robert Beeching, Patricia Garrett, Laurel Wagner, Luisa Kreisberg, Dave, Ben and Leah Wasserman, Marjorie Neikrug, George Alpert, Cecile Fine and Ruth Becker for their encouragement, assistance and professional advice; to Lois de la Haba, whose expertise in books guided the project through; to my wife Fran and my parents, Lewis and Amy Werner, who believed from the beginning.

All these persons and their love made *Reflections of Winter* a reality.